BEAT SPEEDING TICKETS

BEAT SPEEDING TICKETS

Advanced speed-conscious driving, strategies and legal defences to keep you and your licence safe

Andrew Werner

VESADIAM

All rights reserved

Copyright © 2023 Andrew Werner

This book is copyright under the Berne Convention.

No part of this book may be stored on a retrieval system or transmitted in any form or by whatever means without the prior written consent of the publisher. This book may not be lent, resold, hired out or otherwise disposed of by way of trade in any form, binding or cover other than in which it is published, without the prior written consent of the publishers.

Published by Vesadiam, 2023
https://vesadiam.com

ISBN 978-0-9559112-3-1

British Library Cataloguing in Publication Data:

A catalogue record for this book is available from the British Library

Printed and bound by Lightning Source,
England and USA

This book is dedicated to Paul Smith, founder of *Safe Speed*, and to my mother Rosalind, whose ownership of an orange Hillman Imp in the 1970s was instrumental in my learning to swear.

I spent a lot of money on booze, birds and fast cars. The rest I just squandered.

- George Best

Contents

1 Preface 10

2 Background 12

    Introduction 12

    Why do motorists speed? 15

    Safe speeds.. 17

    Setting speed limits 19

    Speed camera enforcement 20

    Enforcement effectiveness.......................... 22

3 Avoidance.. 24

    Vehicles, options and accessories................ 24

    Driver training 26

    Driving style and speeding hazards............. 29

        Overtaking................................. 30

        Motorways................................. 31

        Downhill stretches...................... 32

        Following other vehicles 32

        Tailgating.................................. 33

        Leaving built-up zones............... 34

    Driver health and consciousness 35

    Signage.. 36

    Camera location... 37

Vehicle maintenance	38
4 Detection and prosecution	**40**
Police traffic patrols	40
Automatic cameras	41
Conditional offers	42
Insurance and endorsement periods	43
5 Defence	**45**
Technical errors in serving the NIP	48
Driver identity	49
Driving on private land	49
Necessity	50
Inadequate speed limit signposting	50
Errors in speed detection	51
Time limit for prosecution	54
Failure to produce evidence	54
Court appearance	54
Pleading guilty	55
Court penalties	56
6 Further resources	**57**
Speeding and safety	57
General motoring	58
7 Epilogue	**60**

1 Preface

I have been driving for over 40 years: cars, minibuses and trucks, throughout the British Isles and Europe. For over 20 years, I have written technical documentation in many industries, predominantly IT and software. Although an advanced driver and member of IAM RoadSmart, I *have* racked up the odd speeding ticket.

In fact, in November 2021 I received a Notice of Intended Prosecution (NIP) for allegedly driving at 78mph in a 60mph zone. Shocked at the excess speed, I requested photographs, which appeared to show my innocence. A year later, my case finally came to court (I describe what happened in *7: Epilogue*). While preparing for court I did a great deal of research and realised that I might as well turn that research into a book, as much for my own benefit as for others. This is the result.

Although a short book, *Beat Speeding Tickets* encompasses decades of driver training and experience and months of research, comprising virtually all you need to know about the subject. In it, I describe how to avoid speeding and beat erroneously issued speeding tickets. I do not condone dangerous driving, excessive speed, nor breaking the law. Although the book is largely based on the UK landscape in 2023, it has general applicability for other motoring offences, internationally, and hopefully well into the future. It covers both driving and the attendant legal system.

Once issued, it is extremely difficult to beat a speeding ticket. In the vast majority of cases, the best strategy is simply to take the fixed penalty and amend your driving style. This book therefore concentrates on how to avoid getting a speeding ticket in the first place. However, there are several ways, also covered, in which it is possible to beat erroneously issued tickets.

Compared to a speed awareness course, this book, while including similar material (and much more), is significantly cheaper, quicker and more convenient.

The book is divided into four main sections: *Background, Avoidance, Detection and prosecution* and *Defence*.

2 Background

Introduction

Back in the day, although most of us drove much less powerful cars, they were perfectly capable of exceeding speed limits. However, so long as we drove responsibly, we did not need to constantly keep one eye on the speedometer. In fact, for around 20 years, from the 80s to the mid-noughties, not only did I never receive a speeding ticket: I knew no-one who did.

For today's driver it feels like the state is waging a war on motorists. Although we have the safest, most economical, powerful and advanced vehicles ever made, motorists are subject to ever-increasing charges, taxes, penalties and prosecution for an ever-expanding array of offences. The reasons for these are basically revenue, technology and allegedly, safety and environmental concerns.

Revenue: The motorist is an easy target for governments. Speed cameras are a particularly lucrative source of revenue, with some individual cameras making millions per year in fines. Some police forces have even admitted to placing cameras in locations chosen for revenue opportunities rather than crash black spots[1].

Technology now makes it far easier for police to detect motoring offences. The most obvious is speed limit enforcement. There are also cameras to detect going through red traffic lights, bus lane infringement and stopping in a yellow box junction; other emerging technologies even include capabilities such as automatic detection of drunk or tired drivers, drivers using mobile devices whilst at the wheel and occupants not wearing seat belts.

Safety: In 2016, there were nearly 1,800 road deaths recorded in Great Britain[2], and 1.35 million worldwide[3] (plus many serious injuries), every one of which is a tragedy. Fortunately, at least in Great Britain, these figures have been falling steadily from a peak of nearly 8,000 in 1966, despite a huge growth in vehicle use, although there has been something of a plateau since 2013.

---

[1] Road Traffic law: Police Admit to Speed Cameras Being "Greed Cameras": https://www.roadtrafficlaw.com/police-admit-to-greed-cameras

Daily Express: Speed camera locations are chosen to 'increase revenue', says shocking police report: https://www.express.co.uk/life-style/cars/1310258/speed-camera-uk-locations-fine-ticket-revenue-police

[2] Wikipedia/DOT: Killed on British Roads 2016: https://en.wikipedia.org/wiki/Reported_Road_Casualties_Great_Britain#/media/File:Killed_on_British_Roads.png

[3] Wikipedia/WHO: List of countries by traffic-related death rate: https://en.wikipedia.org/wiki/List_of_countries_by_traffic-related_death_rate

This improvement can be attributed to advances in vehicle and road design, better driver training and testing, and arguably, increased enforcement of traffic laws concerning excessive speed, drunk or drugged driving, helmets, seat belts and child restraints.

Decreasing road safety, the trend towards larger and heavier cars, namely electric and sports utility vehicles is *increasing* deaths and injuries. SUVs have poor near-field visibility and appalling handling, being around twice as likely to roll over in a crash than normal cars[4], while electric cars have a disturbing tendency to self-combust, in fires sometimes taking days to extinguish. Although these vehicles may be safe for their occupants, they are more hazardous to other road users due to their increased weight and for SUVs, size and height.

The safety and unintended consequences of greater driver automation such as adaptive cruise control, lane departure warning and pedestrian avoidance systems are complex and beyond the scope of this book.

All said, it is difficult to attribute quantitative casualty reductions to specific safety measures, particularly the rigid enforcement of speed limits.

Environment: In addition to safety targets, most

---

[4] Wikipedia/US National Highway Traffic Safety Administration: https://en.wikipedia.org/wiki/Criticism_of_sport_utility_vehicles

governments have signed up to net (CO2) zero targets, which invariably results in drives to penalise and reduce vehicle use by whatever means, particularly those powered by internal combustion engines. Several UK cities including London now enforce clean air zones, which charge drivers of older and more polluting vehicles per day to enter. Oxford has recently announced restrictions on motoring between different areas of the city. There are rapid growth of bus lanes, cycle lanes, traffic calming road restrictions and low-traffic neighbourhoods.

Finally, it can hardly be denied that driving is simply one more aspect of our lives that is now monitored and controlled ever more closely by an increasingly **technocratic surveillance state**.

Direct **penalties** for motoring offences include mandatory speed awareness courses, penalty points, fines, loss of licence and imprisonment. Indirect adverse effects may include higher insurance costs, loss of employment and more. The higher insurance costs for a driver with penalty points usually far eclipse the direct costs of fines.

WHY DO MOTORISTS SPEED?

All cars can travel at far higher speeds than humans running or cycling; modern cars are vastly more powerful than those of just a few years ago; it is natural to want to take advantage of this capability. Indeed, speed is exhilarating, as expressed in many a fast car review, hence the popularity of motor racing as a sport. Under suitable conditions, it feels like there is not much point tootling along when our car is capable of much higher speeds; indeed, driving at an inappropriately slow speed presents its own hazards.

We may wish to complete our journey in a shorter time, show off our car and driving skills to passengers, or just feel the thrill of acceleration, cornering and speed. We may be late for an appointment. Some cars are so luxurious (in terms of quietness and comfort) that they give the illusion that they are travelling at a much lower speed than they actually are. We may have an emergency. Inexperienced drivers may lack the skill to control their speed; tired or intoxicated drivers may speed simply because their judgement is impaired. We may be unfamiliar with the vehicle. The vehicle's speedometer may be broken or faulty. We may be unaware of the speed limit or assume a few extra mph leeway. Speed limits may be set unrealistically low, such that the car, driver and conditions allow a higher safe speed.

None of these reasons provide an admissible legal defence, although a genuine emergency or faulty speedometer in a loaned vehicle could provide good mitigation for a guilty plea, or reason for clemency if stopped by a traffic officer.

SAFE SPEEDS

Legal speed limits do not necessarily correspond to **safe speeds**, which vary dynamically according to many factors including: the driver's skill, age, consciousness and reaction time; the vehicle and its condition; light and weather conditions; the road, other traffic and presence of hazards, including pedestrians.

Both safe speeds and legal speed limits are related to stopping distances, which increase exponentially with speed. When a vehicle brakes, it is converting kinetic (moving) energy into heat energy.

kinetic energy is half the product of mass times velocity squared.

$KE = ½ MV^2$

Hence sports cars aim to be as light as possible (and have powerful brakes); some classes of large and heavy vehicles have lower legal speed limits and must have speed limiters fitted.

A simple definition of safe speed is that a vehicle should be able to stop before or safely avoid any visible or potential hazard.

For example, for a skilled driver in a capable car on a good two-lane dual carriageway in perfect weather conditions with a junction visible or signposted ahead on the left, the safe speed in the left lane could be 60mph, while a safe speed in the right-hand carriageway might be 100mph. For a novice driver in an old van, these speeds might be

40mph and 50mph respectively. In fog, they could be 15mph and 25mph. In all conditions, the legal speed limit would remain fixed at 70mph, although a police officer could justifiably stop and prosecute any driver travelling in heavy fog at an unsafe speed such as 50mph.

Another example: A suburban road with cars parked both sides (with the potential hazards of hidden pedestrians suddenly running into the road). With oncoming traffic, in the left-hand lane, a safe speed might be 15mph; with no oncoming traffic, in the middle of the road, a safe speed could be 20mph. In both cases, the legal speed limit might be 30mph.

On most roads, the *safe speed* therefore continually changes according to conditions while the *legal speed limit* remains constant. Probably the most common and fundamental reason why drivers exceed speed limits is this anomaly between safe speed and legal speed limits.

Many rural roads are subject to a national speed limit of 60mph, although in some places, a safe speed may be no more than 10mph. On the other hand, some roads have excessively low speed limits, where most skilled drivers, in good conditions and left to their own judgement, would drive at appreciably higher speeds.

You can make a good case that it would be better and safer to invest in enhanced driver training rather than rigid speed limit enforcement, and to allow drivers to concentrate more on the road ahead rather than their speedometer. However we may wish and campaign for such a situation, we must deal with the motoring and legal landscape as it stands.

SETTING SPEED LIMITS

Speed limits have existed almost since the invention of the motor car and are largely set according to road type: In the UK, motorways and dual carriageways 70mph; single carriageways 60mph; urban/suburban roads 30mph. Speed limits may be reduced due to tight bends, a history of crashes, hidden dips or other hazards such as buildings and junctions. Additionally, temporary and/or dynamic limits may be imposed to mitigate congestion or protect road workers.

The 70mph motorway limit was set in 1965; since then, there have been unsuccessful attempts to raise it to 80mph. Motorway speed limits are actually lowering in many places, and some motorways such as London's orbital M25 implement dynamic speed limits shown on overhead gantries to avoid traffic 'bunching' and the attendant congestion.

Since 1990 there has been a growing movement to reduce suburban speed limits to 20mph and enforce lower speeds through traffic calming measures such as bumps, curves and other obstructions, in order to reduce pedestrian fatalities. Although from signage 20mph limits look like any other, they are usually advisory only and are not enforced.

Speed limits on semi-private roads such as driveways to hotels are often set to extremely low levels such as 10mph. Legal enforcement of such very low limits is questionable, but driving laws apply equally to any road with public access such as a supermarket car park.

The setting of speed limits sometimes involves public consultation and a statistical analysis of vehicle speeds. It is generally considered that the appropriate speed limit for a section of road is that where 85% of traffic travels at that speed or lower – the 85th percentile speed.

Speed camera enforcement

The first roadside-based speed detection device was invented by racing driver Maurice Gatsonides in 1960s Holland; it used rubber tubes on the road to calculate speed. His company, Gatsometer B.V. went on to develop and market speed detection technology. The first British speed camera, a Gatso, was installed on the A316 over Twickenham bridge in 1992, where it detected drivers exceeding the 40mph limit by over 20mph! Modern cameras are generally set to a margin of around 10% + 2mph, although this varies.

In March 2000, the UK Government published a White Paper, *Tomorrow's Roads – Safer for Everyone*, which promised considerable reductions in road accident injuries by 2010. A pilot speed camera scheme in eight areas appeared to result in an approximate 50% reduction in killed and seriously injured (KSI) figures. This prompted a national roll-out and the mass deployment of speed cameras across the UK throughout the noughties, which has continued to this day.

Britain now has thousands of fixed and mobile cameras. Detection methods vary: some cameras photograph cars against marks on the road while others use radar, laser or infra-red light. Average speed cameras are installed in pairs and measure speeds between two points, usually on motorways and 'A' roads.

The three most common speed camera systems are *Gatso* (rear facing, radar operated), *Truvelo* (front facing, either laser or sensors beneath road surfaces) and *SPECS* (front facing, speed-over-distance). Only Gatso-type cameras flash.

Cameras may be fixed automatic installations or operated by police traffic patrols or roadside operators in vans. Police traffic patrols may be in marked or unmarked cars.

Automatic camera data is analysed by enforcement staff, who then send a letter to the vehicle's registered keeper demanding to know who was driving at the time of the alleged offence, followed by an NIP addressed to the driver.

In the 2000s, when speed cameras became ubiquitous, there were various campaigns against their deployment, including some vigilante vandalism. These campaigns are now much less active, with the motoring public largely resigned to speeding enforcement or concerned with more pressing matters.

Enforcement effectiveness

There has been much controversy over the effectiveness of speeding enforcement with regard to safety. Studies have shown conflicting results.

Some anomalies concern the definition of a speeding driver. There is clearly a massive difference between an intoxicated joyrider evading a police chase and driving at 70mph in a 30 zone, and a responsible driver on the same road doing 40mph because the road's speed limit has been set too low, at least for driving in good conditions. Studies which equate the two under a simple heading of 'speeding' produce skewed and inaccurate conclusions.

A study conducted by the London School of Economics found that from 1992 to 2016, traffic enforcement cameras reduced accidents by between 17% and 39%, while reducing fatalities by between 58% and 68%. Similarly, an RAC Foundation report found that the number of serious collisions near

551 fixed speed cameras reduced by 27% after the cameras were put into action[5].

Critics however have vigorously disputed such studies, citing such statistical phenomena as 'revision to the mean' and the adverse unintended side effects on driving caused by vigilant speed limit enforcement – largely distraction and poor driving caused by slavish adherence to inappropriate speed limits. The late Paul Smith of *Safe Speed* performed exhaustive analyses of accident statistics[6] and concluded that the proportion of injury crashes involving any speeding vehicle nationally was only 5% - not the 'one third' previously claimed. In March 2007, he learned via a Freedom of Information request that the speed camera side effects research (announced in May 2005) had been axed. He said that it was inconceivable that the side effects did not cause more than 25 deaths per year (versus 25 lives supposedly saved), and likely over 1,000, meaning that speed cameras are making road safety dramatically worse.

---

[5] Politics.co.uk: https://www.politics.co.uk/reference/speed-cameras/
[6] Side Effects of Speed Cameras and Speed Camera Policy: http://www.safespeed.org.uk/sideeffects.pdf

3 Avoidance

Prevention is far better than cure and speeding tickets are extremely difficult to challenge. This section covers ways to avoid speeding, improve your driving, detect speed cameras, and thus avoid crashes, near-misses and prosecution.

Vehicles, options and accessories

Commercial drivers usually have little choice as to the vehicle they drive, but most car drivers do. Our choice includes many factors including new or used, and if so, age; price of purchase, finance terms, fuel type, safety, brand, style, size, power, economy, gadgetry and degree of comfort.

Some vehicles have a configurable alarm for high speeds. Some have options for head-up displays, which project the speedometer and other information to the windshield.

You can also get after-market gadgets and options such as GPS sat-nav systems, speed camera detectors and dashboard cameras (dash cams, highly recommended), which record video and speed. Most sat-navs show the speed limit as part of their map display. While speed camera detection is legal, laser jammers are not.

From May 2022, new car models in the EU have been required to have a variety of new safety technologies, including speed limiters and systems to monitor the driver's attention levels. There must also be automatic emergency braking, lane assist, backup cameras and an event data recorder similar to an aircraft's 'black box' to store information from before a crash. These technologies will be included in some form on all cars sold in Europe at least, including the UK, not just within the EU.

Intelligent Speed Assist (ISA) dynamically limits speed according to legal limits, albeit allowing brief excursions over the speed limit. The technology detects speed limits by a combination of GPS linked to a road map database and traffic sign recognition cameras. The UK's Department of Transport however has stated that it expects limiters 'to give drivers feedback when the speed limit is exceeded rather than limiting the speed' with a reduction in engine power.

From May 2024, the EU will require *all* new cars to incorporate the technology.

In addition, car manufacturers, led by Volvo, are now starting to incorporate absolute speed limiters set at 180km/h (112mph) on new cars.

Speedometers usually slightly over-read vehicle speeds by up to 10% + 6mph. This is by design, to account for variances in tyre wear and inflation, and to ensure that drivers adhering to speed limits by using the speedometer do not break them inadvertently. You can check your speedometer by comparing its reading to that of a sat-nav device or app at various speeds, on level roads. It is safest to do this with a friend in the passenger seat operating the check device.

Beware of very powerful cars, which have become much more numerous over recent years (many electric cars have dizzying acceleration). Beware also of cars with highly capable sports suspension, limousine comfort, and especially hi-tech adaptive suspension. It's not that you should not buy or drive such cars but do be aware of their capabilities. Such cars cry out to be driven fast, and the obviously flashy ones might as well have a target painted on their rapidly diminishing rear.

Sports cars with harsh suspension do give the driver a more accurate feeling of speed, but encourage speeding round corners; conversely, limousines may handle like boats but be so comfortable that they feel like they are doing much lower than actual speeds.

Be aware of what you are driving, and if it's a supercar, book track time to play; don't do it on a public highway.

Driver training

In the UK, drivers have had to hold a driving licence since 1903 and had to pass a test since 1935. This test has understandably evolved over the years to encompass modern vehicle and road conditions. It is now divided into theory and test parts. Drivers of large/heavy goods and passenger vehicles must pass additional tests. The Highway Code has been published since 1931 and had regular revisions ever since. All drivers should acquire and be acquainted with the current Highway Code.

As with any skill, proficiency is a combination of training and practice. One part of this is to cultivate a good sense of your particular vehicle's speed without even looking at the speedometer.

It is also worth being aware of the Dunning-Kruger effect: *a cognitive bias whereby people with limited knowledge or competence in a given intellectual or social domain greatly overestimate their own knowledge or competence in that domain relative to objective criteria or to the performance of their peers or of people in general*[7]. What that means in this context is that most drivers regard themselves as being over-average in terms of driving skills, which is obviously impossible. Especially if you are a newly qualified, occasional or inexperienced driver, appreciate the fact and drive accordingly, i.e., with more caution. Whoever you are, do not be under the illusion that you are a perfect driver, and always show consideration to other road users.

There is no substitute for hours behind the wheel, but there are additional driving courses and tests well worth taking including:

---

[7] Encyclopaedia Britannica: https://www.britannica.com/science/Dunning-Kruger-effect

- **Pass Plus**: Specifically designed for new drivers, this six-hour multi-session course includes situations not well covered in learner driver lessons such as rural roads, complicated city situations, bad weather, night driving, dual carriageways and motorways.
- **Advanced Driver**: Provided by IAM RoadSmart (formerly the Institute of Advanced Motorists) and modelled on the police advanced driving system (the System of Car Control), this course teaches additional on-road knowledge and skills, above and beyond what is taught when you learn to drive. It takes between 6-12 sessions with a certified observer and concludes with a test.
- **Skid pan training**: You can experience skids driving front- and rear-wheel-drive cars on an oiled slippery surface and learn how to control and rectify loss of traction (my major conclusion from this course was to avoid such situations like the plague).
- Especially since you are reading this book, you may have taken a **speed awareness course**. These courses may be offered to motorists who have been detected breaking speed limits by a small margin, as an alternative to a fine and penalty points. They include material on stopping distances and fatality probabilities for pedestrians hit at different speeds. For example, a pedestrian hit by a car at 30mph

has a 20% chance of being killed. At 35mph, this increases to 33%. Another particularly useful subject covered is speed limit signage, to which you should always pay close attention. Learning never stops. Even if you have undergone some form of additional driver training in the past, it is always worth keeping your skills up to date with continued training. There are many other resources worth seeking out about advanced driving techniques.

Driving style and speeding hazards

One of the most important ways to avoid speeding, and hence tickets, is to adjust your driving style. Rather than always trying to go as fast as possible, chill! That does not mean driving so slowly as to be an annoyance to other road users; rather, it means allowing enough time for your journey so as to not be in a rush and enjoying your time behind the wheel so far as possible, for example by enjoying the scenery and/or listening to music, audiobooks or podcasts while driving, driving at a legal and safe speed, and appreciating the fact that you cannot always travel or overtake at the speed limit or speed limit plus 'x', whether because of traffic, other hazards, road conditions or speed limits.

You may also use your car's dashboard to show average economy/MPG per trip (aiming to keep it as high as possible), drive in 'eco' or comfort mode (rather than sports), or install an app such as DriveScore, which rates your driving, penalising your score for reckless habits like rapid acceleration, braking, cornering, speeding and phone distraction (I allegedly drive like a hooligan, being guilty of the first three, but can't see the point of driving a fast car with harsh suspension if you can't take advantage of its strengths. Ah, well).

This section discusses the psychology of speeding, particularly with regard to common speeding hazard situations (which often occur in combination, for example overtaking in traffic on a motorway).

Overtaking

Of all situations, overtaking represents probably the greatest temptation to speed. Overtaking is inherently hazardous, since for a short time your vehicle may be on the wrong side of the road. Alternatively, you may be in a stretch of road with a short overtaking lane. In both cases, the natural and rational urge is to complete the manoeuvre as quickly as possible. You may feel like simply downshifting and putting your foot to the floor until you have passed the slower vehicle then returning to your lane; before the widespread deployment of speed cameras, this was for most drivers the usual *modus operandi*. Unfortunately, this way, it is all too easy to massively exceed the speed limit; police are on the look-out for exactly this situation. In fact, they often monitor speeds at the exact spots where overtaking is possible.

The fact that you were overtaking, and only speeding for a short time is no defence. The only way to overtake without risking prosecution is to keep an eye on your speedometer and keep within the speed limit, however dangerous and counter-intuitive this may be. Thus, in many cases, overtaking may be physically feasible but legally impossible.

Motorways

It is easy to be tempted to speed on motorways and other dual-carriageway high-speed roads, especially in good conditions and when free of other traffic. Needless to say, although conditions may be similar to an unrestricted German autobahn, all UK motorways are subject to a maximum speed limit of 70mph, often much lower.

Some motorways ('smart' or otherwise) employ dynamic variable speed limits; it is essential to note these and comply.

Motorways and dual carriageways are well equipped with speed cameras, often placed strategically where it feels natural to go faster than the speed limit. Assume leeway at your peril.

Downhill stretches

The sun is shining, your favourite tune is playing on the radio, the road is clear and you have just passed the peak of a hill, cruising happily down a long downhill stretch. You glance down and whoops! You're doing 100mph. Unfortunately, so is the the unmarked police car with flashing blue lights behind you. Don't let exuberance mar your judgement.

Following other vehicles

Just as our behaviour can be influenced by others in social situations, so it can on the road. In traffic, it is natural to follow the vehicle in front at the same speed. Many vehicles now incorporate adaptive cruise control, which automates the practice. In most cases, especially in heavy traffic, vehicles will travel at the speed limit or less, especially since drivers have now been thoroughly conditioned to do so by speed limit enforcement. This may not always be the case however, especially when following a single vehicle. Some situations of greatest temptation are motorway driving and driving at night.

On a congested motorway it can be difficult to change lane; it may feel as if one has no choice between being stuck in a convoy of slow-moving vehicles in lanes one and two or sucked into a procession of speeding cars in lane three. Do not be pressured; keep to the highway code. Drive at the maximum safe and legal speed in the leftmost lane necessary, pulling over into slower lanes only when possible, allowing speeding cars to pass you.

Nighttime driving on unlit roads is also stressful, with sometime blinding from oncoming traffic's headlights and the frequent need to adjust your own headlights from dipped to full beam (unless you have automatic headlight technology). Again, it is easy to get sucked into closely following the vehicle in front. For one thing, this has the advantage that you can drive solely on dipped beam, with no need to switch back and forth between full and dipped. This is a good strategy so long at the vehicle you are following is doing a safe and legal speed. Do not be tempted into exceeding the speed limit or safe speed – which at nighttime may well be lower than the posted speed limit.

Some roads such as the old Mersey Tunnel (Queensway) have narrow, twisting lanes, where it feels (and is) safer to keep up with other traffic rather than be overtaken closely. In such circumstances, you have to judge carefully between the hazards of speeding versus potential collision.

Tailgating

An important aspect of safe driving, if you are in traffic, is to leave sufficient space between you and the vehicle in front. If the vehicle in front of you does a sudden stop, you need to be able to stop safely, within the space available.

If you are followed closely by another vehicle (tailgated), there is a natural inclination to speed up, which can easily lead to breaking the speed limit, crashes and/or prosecution. Being tailgated is definitely not an acceptable defence!

The safest way to deal with tailgating is, if you are following other traffic, back off yourself a little until you have established extra space between you and the vehicle in front. That way, if it does suddenly stop, *you* can stop smoothly, with less danger of being rear-ended. If you are on a multi-lane road, move left when possible, allowing the tailgater to overtake you. You cannot control its speed, and if the driver wants to break the speed limit and risk prosecution, let him. The important thing is to avoid crashes and speeding tickets.

LEAVING BUILT-UP ZONES

Sometimes, when leaving a built-up area with a 30 or 40mph limit, there is an appreciable distance covered by the low speed limit before the national speed limit is signposted. It feels natural, with the built-up area behind you, once you see the national speed limit sign, to put your foot down and accelerate.

Beware! Feels natural, but is not legal. Police routinely monitor speeds in such places. Always wait until you have actually passed the higher speed limit signs before accelerating.

Driver health and consciousness

Intoxication, tiredness and distraction all have massive adverse effects on a driver's ability to drive safely, as do many health conditions.

If you drink or take other recreational drugs, never do so when driving, nor drive the morning after a heavy session, when you may still be intoxicated and your driving ability impaired. It used to be acceptable to drink a certain amount and drive, but not anymore: any amount of alcohol or drug impairs reaction time and driving ability. It is very difficult to stop drinking after a small amount or gauge the legally permissible amount of alcohol in your bloodstream, even with a personal breathalyser. Driving while intoxicated often results in increased risk-taking and speeds. If you do crash after drinking even a 'moderate' amount of alcohol, you will never know if your drinking contributed to the crash. If you have killed or seriously injured someone, the guilt will stay with you for life.

If prescribed drugs by a doctor, always ask if they may impair your driving ability and avoid driving if necessary.

If you require glasses, you must always wear them whilst driving. You need to be able to see the road ahead, any hazards and your dashboard instruments, including speedometer.

If you suffer from a chronic condition which may impair your driving, take your doctor's advice and if advised, you must inform the DVLA.

Never drive when tired; always take regular breaks on long journeys.

Avoid distraction, such as animated conversations with passengers or loud, fast bass-heavy music. Wait until hazards have passed before adjusting non-essential controls like climate control or music. Always stop before programming a sat-nav, or use voice control.

Texting whilst driving is one of the most irresponsible and dangerous things you can possibly do: The [US] National Safety Council reports that cell phone use while driving leads to 1.6 million crashes each year; texting while driving is **six times** more likely to cause an accident than driving drunk[8]. Never touch a mobile phone when driving.

SIGNAGE

Speed limits are normally marked by circular red-ringed signs showing either a speed in miles per hour or a black circle with diagonal line – indicating the national speed limit.

Changes in speed limits are shown with signs at both sides of the road. In Scotland there are often 3-2-1 countdown signs. For speed limits lower than national, there are regular reminder signs on the left.

---

[8] https://www.edgarsnyder.com/car-accident/cause-of-accident/cell-phone/cell-phone-statistics.html

Some speed limits are dynamic, for example 20mph when lights are flashing – around schools, and on some motorway gantries.

Not all speed limits need to be signposted; for example, if a road has regular lamp posts, then its default speed limit is 30mph. National speed limit roads may vary between unsignposted 60 and 70mph limits as they change between single- and dual-carriageway (NOT number of lanes). They may also change to lower, signposted limits for certain sections.

Inadequate speed limit signposting can form the basis of a legal defence for speeding.

Camera location

Ever since the advent of speed cameras, motorists have sought warnings of their use. Indeed, the Automobile Association (AA) was originally formed (as The Motorists' Mutual Association) in 1905 to warn motorists of police speed traps! Drivers sometimes flash oncoming traffic to warn of speed traps, but this itself is of dubious legality (although warning a non-speeding driver is perfectly legal, warning a speeding driver is illegal since you would be aiding and abetting someone getting away with a crime and interfering with the police in the course of their duty).

Seeking to know speed camera locations is a perfectly legitimate and legal activity; since speed cameras are supposed to be located in accident hot-spots, such knowledge should warn motorists of especially hazardous stretches of road. Whether located at accident black-spots or not, cameras are often placed where drivers tend to speed.

You can discover speed camera locations by various means: visually, from discussion with other drivers, by online lists and maps, through smartphone apps and options in some sat-nav and dash-cam devices and apps. There are also specialised detectors, which may be well worth it, especially if you have already accumulated penalty points or cannot live without your licence. You can find such devices by internet searches with terms like 'speed camera detector' or 'radar detector'.

Vehicle maintenance

It is imperative to keep your vehicle in good condition, and indeed an offence to drive an unroadworthy vehicle, even if it has a current MOT, even if its upkeep is supposedly another's responsibility such as your employer or a hire company. The annual MOT is a useful check, but you must regularly check yourself the condition of safety-critical equipment such as windscreen washers, tyres, lights and brakes.

Have your vehicle regularly serviced; quickly investigate and rectify any faults such as strange noises or uneven suspension. Improper tyre pressures, brake and suspension faults may significantly increase stopping distances. I have even known cases where a vehicle has passed MOTs with a non-functioning speedometer. Obviously, such a fault is both illegal and may result in inadvertent speeding.

4 Detection and prosecution

There is little like the feeling of dread when receiving a speeding ticket, especially if you already have penalty points on your driving licence. Speeding tickets are very hard to defend, which is why this book strongly advises preventative measures.

As mentioned previously in the section *Speed Camera Enforcement*, there are basically two ways in which you can be caught speeding: police traffic patrol and automatic camera.

There are minor but sometimes significant differences in motoring law between the countries of the United Kingdom which you should be aware of. For example in Northern Ireland, learner and restricted drivers (who have passed their test within the last 12 months) are restricted to 45mph.

Police traffic patrols

Patrolling traffic police may stop a speeding driver and issue a fixed penalty ticket or advise of intended prosecution directly at the roadside.

If you are accused of a crime, the best option generally is to say nothing to the police. However, if you are stopped by a traffic patrol, you must cooperate to some degree, at least confirming your name, address and sobriety.

After checking your name and address, the

police will generally ask you if you know how fast you were driving. You do not need to incriminate yourself by admitting to driving above the speed limit. However, you should be polite and cooperative (without necessarily admitting guilt), in order to minimise or avoid penalties.

If you have only exceeded the speed limit by a small amount, you may escape with a warning. However, traffic police generally have targets to fulfil, and if you have exceeded the permissible leeway, they are likely to issue you with a fixed penalty, either on-the-spot or by post later. If you were driving excessively fast, they may give you notice of prosecution in court.

Of course, feel free to use all the charm and excuses you like. If you have a genuine emergency such as transporting someone seriously ill or injured to hospital, the police may be sympathetic and even give you an escort. Obviously, under no circumstances try to bribe a police officer, since this is both highly unlikely to be successful, and a much more serious offence than speeding, indeed criminal.

Automatic cameras

Most speeding drivers are detected by automatic camera. The next step is a letter from a 'safety camera partnership' to the vehicle's registered keeper demanding an admission of who was driving at the time of the alleged offence (under section 172 of the Road Traffic Act 1988). You must reply within 28 days. Failure to disclose the driver's identity is an offence in itself. You may not know who was driving, for example if your car was stolen. If so, you must state this on the Section 172 notice or an accompanying letter. If you do not reply, you can be prosecuted for this as well as the alleged speeding offence, with penalties up to a £1,000 fine and six points or disqualification.

Conditional offers

Whether you were stopped by traffic police, or detected by automatic camera and have submitted a section 172 notice that you were driving, the next stage is an NIP. Unless your alleged speed was very high, this will be accompanied by a fixed penalty offer of around three penalty points and a £100 fine. In most cases, this will be preferable to court.

Although the fixed penalty notice generally demands a response within 28 days, it is not unknown for this to be resent, giving you another 7- or 14-days grace, although you should not count on this. If you are a little late, reply accepting the fixed penalty anyway, together with a letter explaining your tardiness. As well as paying the fine, you must also send your licence for endorsement.

Insurance and endorsement periods

Insurance companies do of course charge higher premiums for drivers with penalty points or endorsements on their licence, reflecting the higher risk that such drivers represent.

You have a legal obligation to tell your car insurance provider all relevant information about a policy's drivers and vehicles, including any driver motoring offences.

Withholding or falsifying such information may invalidate your insurance, which in itself could represent another offence. Your insurance provider could even cancel your insurance, which would make getting insurance in the future extremely difficult and expensive.

Should you be involved in a collision, be liable for damages, have invalid insurance and have assets such as a property, you could be ruined.

You must therefore inform your insurance company as soon as you have accepted a fixed penalty or been found guilty of a motoring offence. Do not wait until renewal. You cannot necessarily get away with simply changing your insurance company at renewal since companies share information through databases.

Speeding offences and their attendant penalty points remain active on your driving licence for four years from the date of the offence, whereupon they become 'spent'. Other, more serious motoring offences such as drink driving remain on your driving license for 11 years from the date of conviction.

You must inform your insurer of any motoring offences within the past five years only; you do not have to declare offences older than five years.

5 DEFENCE

If you genuinely doubt that you were speeding, examine whatever evidence you can discover as soon as you can. Use the period between receiving a Section 172 notice and NIP to maximise the time you have for investigation. This will enable you to better understand your case and whether it is worth defending.

- If you have a dash-cam, examine the video record at the time of the alleged offence.
- If possible, identify, visit and photograph the section of road where you were allegedly caught speeding. If this is impractical, use Google street view.
- Request photographs from the police showing your alleged speeding.

If you have a genuine defence such as an emergency, you should first write to the enforcement body and request that they drop the prosecution. Should they refuse (highly likely), you may still have the option of accepting a fixed penalty.

If you are sure that you have a good defence, write to the enforcement body outlining why you think you are innocent. If they drop your case, all well and good. More likely, they will reject your defence and give you another chance to pay a fixed penalty within 7-14 days.

If you do not hear from the enforcement body for

a long time, do not assume that they have dropped your case. Court proceedings may have begun without your knowledge. It may be 12 months from the date of your alleged offence before you receive a court summons.

Once you receive a court summons, you have the option of pleading not guilty or guilty with mitigating circumstances. Whatever, you must reply promptly, within the period specified.

If your case does go to court, your best chance of winning is to involve a specialist solicitor at an early stage. Your solicitor will be able to review the evidence and advise you on the best course of action. Such legal representation is not cheap however, typically costing well over £1,000. There is seldom legal aid available, and if you win your case, you may not be able to recover all your costs.

Although you may be able to obtain copies of photographic evidence before deciding whether to contest the charge or accept a fixed penalty, obtaining video evidence is much more difficult, and usually only possible after you have received a summons to court. Even then, the PPS (Public Prosecution Service) will generally refuse to give you a copy of the DVD or video file electronically. You and/or your solicitor may have to attend a police station to view the footage.

If you plead not guilty, the prosecution must prove beyond reasonable doubt that you were driving a motor vehicle on a public road or place and exceeding the speed limit.

The photographic and/or video speed camera evidence will show the vehicle speeding, but this may not necessarily be sufficient to identify the driver.

Do not attempt flimsy defences such as:
- only exceeding the speed limit by a small amount,
- overtaking,
- faulty speedometer,
- In a hurry.

Leeway is at the discretion of the officer or police force, and although it is generally set at 10% plus a few mph, the police can prosecute for even 1mph over the speed limit. It is the driver's responsibility to ensure that their speedometer is working, although a slightly under-reading speedometer could provide good mitigating circumstances for a guilty plea.

Legitimate defences are:
- Technical errors in serving the NIP,
- Driver identity,
- Driving on private land,
- Necessity,
- Time limit for prosecution,
- Failure to produce evidence,
- Inadequate speed limit signposting,
- Errors in speed detection.

Technical errors in serving the NIP

The NIP must be served within 14 days of the alleged speeding offence. Late delivery is a grey area, but it certainly worked for David Beckham, who in 2018 employed celebrity lawyer Nick Freeman - aka 'Mr Loophole' to successfully argue that his NIP had been delivered one day late[9].

However, if the NIP follows an accident or the DVLA had not been informed of the correct registered keeper then the NIP may legitimately be served late. If you are not the registered keeper (for example in the case of a hire car) then there may also be reasonable delay in sending you the NIP.

The NIP must contain the following details:
- The offence for which prosecution is being considered (e.g., speeding),
- The time and date of the alleged offence,
- The vehicle alleged to be involved,
- The location of alleged offence,
- A signature (whether typed or printed).

If the NIP is late or any of these details are missing or incorrect, then it is invalid. You may well be able to state this to the safety camera partnership and entirely escape penalties.

If you are stopped by the Police and are not

---

[9] https://www.dailymail.co.uk/news/article-6213539/David-Beckhams-celebrity-lawyer-Mr-Loophole-arrives-court-fight-stars-speeding-charge.html

warned that you may be prosecuted for an offence by an officer in uniform, any postal requisition sent to you outside the 14-day limit may also be invalid.

Driver identity

With automatic speeding detection, someone else may have been driving. The camera may have caught another vehicle with cloned number plates. If you were sharing driving with a companion such as your spouse, you may be genuinely unsure as to who was driving. You could have sold the vehicle. You can reply stating this; however photographic evidence may show the driver's identity.

You may have to provide proof that you were elsewhere/not driving at the time of the alleged offence. Be aware that false statements about the identity of the driver constitute conspiracy to pervert the course of justice, which is a far more serious offence than speeding where conviction often results in a custodial sentence.

Driving on private land

Speeding and other motoring laws apply to any place where the public has access, for example farm roads, non-adopted roads and hotel access driveways. In order to use this defence, the location would have to be really private, in the sense of no public access. To prove this, you could show maps and photos. On the other hand, it is highly unlikely that you would be caught speeding on truly private land anyway.

Necessity

If you had a genuine emergency such as driving yourself or a passenger to hospital for urgent medical attention or even being pursued by paparazzi then you may have had a valid reason for speeding and should be able to get the ticket dismissed, preferably before it gets to court. You would clearly need evidence.

Inadequate speed limit signposting

As described earlier, road types have default speed limits where no explicit signposting is strictly necessary.

If though, you have been caught on an unlit single carriageway road with a 30, 40 or 50mph limit, or a dual carriageway/motorway with a limit below 70mph, it may well be worth checking the signposting. Signs are sometimes obstructed, obscured, missing or inadequate. If this is the case, which you can check yourself, then you have a valid defence. You should take photographs or video showing the inadequate signposting.

Similarly, the speed limit may have been imposed without all necessary legal procedure being followed. When the speed limit of a road is changed, there has to be an order made and approved by the local council. The time frame that applies to all changes is precisely recorded and noted. Looking into this is more protracted, and you might well need a solicitor to investigate.

ERRORS IN SPEED DETECTION

Despite their sophistication, speed guns may sometimes give erroneously high readings.

In 2005, the BBC program *Inside Out* investigated one of the most popular laser speed detection guns used by police forces in the US and UK[10]. In the program, a pair of American specification LTI 20-20 guns, manufactured by Laser Technology Inc. of Colorado, pointed at the same moving vehicle but recorded substantially different speeds.

The hosts of the BBC program were able to clock a stationary car at 6mph. In tests of a moving vehicle, the laser gun produced erroneous readings almost a third of the time, displaying speeds that were off by as much as 26mph.

The source of the error is well-known: cosine slip. When the aiming point of the laser gun, which is designed to be hand-held, moves or 'slips' across the target vehicle, an extra distance is either added to or subtracted from the speed calculation. A tiny

---

[10] https://www.thenewspaper.com/news/06/649.asp

movement can add up to a substantial difference. Engineering Professor John Brignell described the amount of motion needed to cause a slip error at a distance of 500 metres: "Very roughly, without doing any calculations, we are talking about the camera moving about the thickness of a human hair."

In 2007, A Daily Mail investigation found similar problems with the LTI 20-20 Ultralyte speed gun prone to 'wild' errors[11]. Specifically, a wall was found to travel at 44mph, an empty road 33mph, a parked car 22mph, and a slow-moving bicycle at 66mph.

So, you may be able to argue that a handheld speed gun picked up another vehicle's speed or that it was being moved while taking the reading. In addition, reflective surfaces can interfere with obtaining an accurate reading. However, these BBC and Daily Mail investigations are now rather old, and technology has undoubtedly moved on in the intervening years; a defence solely based on these investigations is unlikely to convince the magistrate.

Hand-held speed guns are supposed to be aimed at a vehicle's number plate, and you may be able to check this by looking at centre cross-hairs on a photograph, or draw your own. Police though are

---

[11] https://www.dailymail.co.uk/news/article-365563/The-great-speed-gun-scandal.html

extremely cagey about releasing speed gun operating manuals and have denied Freedom of Information requests to do so.

You may also claim that a camera had not been properly maintained and calibrated (both before and after detection). Typically, witness statements included with a summons include such details; if these are missing then this may be an avenue worth pursuing.

While snapshot photos showing speed may be open to argument, video footage showing high speeds over several seconds is very difficult to dispute.

In practice, to show an erroneously high speed camera reading, you would really need to find some solid evidence such as distance markers (witness marks) on the road combined with the police evidence photographs. In one case from 2014, a driver beat a speeding ticket by showing that road markings used to detect his speed were three inches too short.

If you have a dash-cam device, you should replay the alleged speeding episode to confirm your speed. If your dash-cam does show a significantly lower speed, you might have it checked and calibrated to increase the weight of its evidence.

Time limit for prosecution

Many motoring offences (including speeding) are summary only which means they can only be tried in a magistrates' court. These are subject to an overall time limit within which to bring proceedings of six months. This time limit runs from the date of the alleged offence to the police beginning court proceedings, not the date of a summons. You will need to examine the summons paperwork carefully to find this start date.

If the police took longer than six months to begin prosecution, then you should **request the magistrate to dismiss the case**.

Failure to produce evidence

A summons will typically include wording along the lines of "If there is anything which might assist your defence as set out in this statement, it will be disclosed to you" together with a list of the evidence. If you request such evidence but the prosecution cannot or does not provide it at or by your next court appearance, then again you should **request the magistrate to dismiss the case**.

Court appearance

Appearing in court is a very stressful business.

The magistrates' court is less formal than a crown court. Nevertheless, prepare and dress well, and behave politely. You can address the magistrate simply as Sir or Madam. Ensure all your paperwork and evidence is well organised. In addition to all the statements and evidence, you must bring your full driving licence and a means (income) form.

If you plead not guilty, be prepared to return to court a few times. The prosecution may need time to produce evidence then to arrange witness appearances. Once you have received all the evidence against you, if you are still pleading not guilty, you must provide a defence statement to the court laying out your basic defence arguments. The magistrate will explain when you need to provide this.

If you are representing yourself, prepare a list of questions for each witness – notably the police officer, speed camera operator and/or back-office investigator. Your witness questions must be respectful and relevant.

As noted above, if you find discrepancies with the prosecution at any point such as the non-appearance of prosecution witnesses, request that the case be dismissed.

Pleading Guilty

If, despite your best efforts, you find the prosecution evidence to be overwhelmingly against you, always be prepared to change your plea to guilty. If your case is unwinnable, this should reduce the penalty.

You must also submit your personal financial circumstances form and surrender your driving licence for endorsement

You should also state the reasons for your speeding, why you should not be heavily punished and any mitigating circumstances. If you are at risk of losing your licence (e.g., if you already have points on your licence), outline the consequences should this happen (such as losing your job).

The magistrate should take these factors into account when sentencing.

COURT PENALTIES

Court penalties for speeding range from fines of £100 and three penalty points up to £1,000 (non-motorway), £2,500 (motorway) and disqualification, depending on the severity of the offence and the offender's income. Penalty points remain on your licence for three years, although you must declare them when applying for insurance for longer, as mentioned earlier.

6 Further resources

Speeding and safety

- **Brake**, "The Road Safety Charity... want[s] a world where everyone is free to move in a safe and healthy way, every day. We work to stop road deaths and injuries, support people affected by road crashes and campaign for safe and healthy mobility for all."
https://www.brake.org.uk/
- The **Safe Speed** campaign, website and forums, founded by the late road safety expert Paul Smith, is one of the original and best places for information on safe driving, speeding and motoring law:
http://www.safespeed.org.uk
- **PePiPoo** ("Helping the motorist get justice") is another excellent resource:
http://www.pepipoo.com

On both Safe Speed and PePiPoo forums, you can get personalised advice about speeding tickets. PePiPoo even includes an 'NIP wizard'.

- The **Alliance of British Drivers** (ABD) is "a voluntary organisation promoting the interests and concerns of Britain's drivers ... promote[s] your views to national and local Government bodies, and provide[s] information to our members and the public. [It] counter[s] the misinformation spread by many people on the use of private vehicles, and promote[s] freedom of choice about how you travel.

The ABD is also represented on the Road User Panel of Transport Focus — the independent transport user watchdog."

https://abd.org.uk

- **IAM RoadSmart** (formerly the Institute of Advanced Motorists) is the UK's largest independent road safety charity. Formed in 1956, it aims to make roads safer by improving driver and rider skills through coaching and education, and offers a range of advanced driving courses.

  It has a network of qualified experts, over 80,000 members and around 180 local groups.

  https://www.iamroadsmart.com

General motoring

- **The Highway Code** encapsulates UK driving law and best practice. Regularly updated, it is essential reading for all road users, particularly drivers.

  https://www.gov.uk/guidance/the-highway-code

- The **AA** (Automobile Association)
  https://www.theaa.com

- The **RAC** (Royal Automobile Club)
  https://www.rac.co.uk

  Both the AA and RAC offer a plethora of useful

motoring and related services including breakdown recovery, servicing, training, finance and information.

7 Epilogue

As mentioned in the preface, I was inspired to write this book after personally receiving and attempting to defend a speeding ticket in 2021/22.

The photographic evidence I requested appeared to show me driving behind a large truck on a single carriageway road. Obviously, the truck would have had a speed limiter installed, so could not have been doing much more than 60mph; nor could I, or I would have crashed into it. I showed the photographs to a speeding defence expert, and he agreed: the speed gun reading must have been wrong due to movement or aiming errors. I wrote to the 'safety camera partnership' and explained. They simply sent me another fixed penalty notice.

Unfortunately, I did not check out the exact stretch of road where I had been snapped. A year later I received a summons, and with court case in progress, viewed the video evidence: It was a two-lane stretch of A-road with overtaking lane where I was clearly both overtaking and speeding. I changed my plea to guilty and fortunately received the minimum penalty. That is why, at the beginning of *Chapter 5, Defence*, I recommend checking out the location of your alleged offence.

If only, back in November 2021, I'd had this book to guide me. Well, I do now, and so do you!

I hope that this book has been useful to help you improve your driving, your safety on the road, avoid speeding tickets and in the event of receiving an unjust ticket, defeat it. Drive safely!

If you have enjoyed or found *Beat Speeding Tickets* useful (or even not!) please review in places like Amazon and Goodreads. Reviews are essential to selling books, and selling books is essential to enabling me to write more...

The End